The freedom riders held a huge meeting in a church in Montgomery.

Martin Luther King rushed to Montgomery to speak. While he spoke, a crowd of angry white people tried to break into the church. King asked his people to sing the black freedom song "We Shall Overcome." As stones and bottles hit the church, the blacks inside sang, "We are not afraid."

T0025844

With special thanks to the Joint Center for

Political and Economic Studies

Copyright © 1969, 1993 by Random House, Inc.

All rights reserved. Published in the United States by Random House Children's Books, a division of Random House, Inc., New York. Originally published in slightly different form by Random House, Inc., in 1969. This revised edition originally published by Random House, Inc., in 1993.

Photo credits: Unless otherwise indicated, all photographs were provided by Flip Schulke. Schulke Archives, pages 32, 54, 55, 58, 73, 81, 94; AP/Wide World Photos, pages 33, 40, 43, 48, 63, 66, 97; The Schomburg Center for Research in Black Culture: New York Public Library, pages 5, 11, 14, 29, 60, 88; UPI/Bettmann Newsphotos, pages iii, 78, 86, 100; The Bettmann Archive, page 22; Black Star Bob Fitch, page 93.

RANDOM HOUSE and colophon are registered trademarks of Random House, Inc.

www.randomhouse.com/kids

Educators and librarians, for a variety of teaching tools, visit us at
www.randomhouse.com/teachers

Library of Congress Cataloging-in-Publication Data
De Kay, James T.
Meet Martin Luther King, Jr. / written by James T. de Kay ; illustrated with photographs.
   p.   cm. — (Landmark books)
SUMMARY: Highlights the life of the man largely responsible for uniting American blacks in the fight for civil rights.
ISBN 978-0-375-80395-6
1. King, Martin Luther, Jr., 1929–1968—Juvenile literature.
2. Afro-Americans—Biography—Juvenile literature.
3. Baptists—United States—Clergy—Biography—Juvenile literature.
[1. King, Martin Luther, Jr., 1929–1968. 2. Civil rights workers.
3. Afro-Americans—Biography.] I. Title. II. Series.
E185.97.K5D43 1989   323.4'092'4—dc19   88-26383

Printed in the United States of America

28 27 26 25 24

First Landmark Books® edition, 2001.

Meet
MARTIN
LUTHER KING, JR.

by James T. de Kay

LANDMARK BOOKS®

RANDOM HOUSE 🏠 NEW YORK

Contents

Martin Luther King, Jr., a man of God and a man of action.

1

Meet Martin Luther King, Jr.

Martin Luther King, Jr., was a fighter. He fought people who used guns and bombs against him. But he did not use a gun. He did not use violence of any kind. He fought with words and ideas. He believed words and ideas could beat guns.

He fought for fair laws. He fought for an end to hate. He fought for a better life for all Americans. Thousands of people knew he was right. Thousands followed him. And slowly America began to change.

Martin Luther King lost his life in the fight to change America. But his words and ideas live on.

Martin was born and grew up in this house.

2
Big Words and a Hard Head

When Martin Luther King, Jr., was born, he didn't yell like most babies. He lay very still. He was so quiet, the doctor thought he was dead.

Smack! The doctor gave the fat baby a hard spank. At last Martin Luther King, Jr., gave his first cry.

The peaceful baby was born at home in Atlanta, Georgia. January 15, 1929, was a cold, gray Tuesday.

Martin Luther King, Jr., was a big name for a little boy. Everyone called him "M. L."

M. L.'s father's name was also Martin Luther King. He was the assistant pastor of the Ebenezer Baptist Church. It was a large church, and he played an important part in the lives of its many members. It was a center of hope for a better life.

M. L.'s mother was Alberta King. Her father, Rev. Adam Daniel Williams, was the head pastor of the church. She had been a teacher before her children were born. M. L. had an older sister, Christine, and a younger brother, Alfred Daniel.

The Kings lived in a large, comfortable house. They had nice clothes. There was always plenty to eat. But M. L. grew up knowing that many people in Atlanta were poor and didn't have these things.

His father's church was a very big part of M. L.'s life. As a tiny boy he sang hymns there. He sang all by himself in front of hundreds of people.

And his father made his children learn verses from the Bible by heart. M. L., Chris-

M. L. (on right) with his parents, grandmother, brother, and sister.

tine, and Alfred Daniel each had to say their Bible verses aloud at dinner. The verses had big words and a special rhythm.

From the time he was a little boy, M. L. loved words. He loved to hear his father speak in church. He would watch the way people listened. He could see how strong words were.

When he was little, he said to his mother, "You just wait and see. I'm going to get me some big words."

M. L. loved to play, too. He was small for his age. But he played hard. Some of his friends thought he played too hard.

One time, when he was five, he was playing on the stairs. Suddenly he slipped and fell. Crash! He dropped 20 feet to the floor. He landed on his head and tumbled into the cellar. But he was not hurt!

Two other times cars smashed into his bicycle. Both times he was thrown to the ground. But he was not hurt either time.

Once he and his brother were playing baseball. His brother swung the bat hard. It slipped out of his hands and hit M. L. on the head. M. L. fell down, but he got right up. Once again he was not hurt!

Years later Martin Luther King thought of all the times he was hit on the head. "God was looking out for me even then," he said with a grin. "He must have given me a hard head."

3

Jim Crow

M. L. was a happy little boy. But when he was about five, something happened that made him very sad. There was a small grocery store across the street from his house. Every day M. L. went over to play with the grocer's two little boys. They were good friends.

Then a strange thing happened. One day M. L. went to play as usual. But the boys didn't come out. Their mother came instead. She said her two boys could never play with M. L. again. She sent him home.

M. L. wanted to cry. He didn't understand. He ran home to his mother and asked what was wrong. Mrs. King sighed and looked sad. She picked him up and put him on her lap. Then she explained.

She said everyone in the grocer's family had light skin. They were called "white" people. But everyone in M. L.'s family had dark skin. They were called "Negroes" or "black" people or "colored" people.

Then she said that some white people didn't like black people. She told him how, long, long ago, whites brought blacks from Africa to America. They made them work in fields as slaves. She told M. L. how cruel some white slave-owners were. They beat the blacks with whips. They bought and sold them like animals.

Then came the Civil War. The Southern states decided to form a separate country with different laws from those of the United States. The states in the North were against slavery. The states in the South were for it.

Many soldiers on both sides were killed

and wounded. A unit of free black soldiers fought and died bravely for the North. After many bloody battles, the North won.

After the war the slaves were set free. But many whites, especially in the South, still treated black people unfairly. They cheated them and did all they could to keep them from getting ahead in life. Sometimes they even killed them.

White people made special laws against blacks. Some whites who didn't like black people called them "Jim Crows." So they called the special laws "Jim Crow laws."

One Jim Crow law said that no black child could go to school with white children. Another said that black people could not eat in restaurants where white people ate. Blacks could not wash their clothes in the laundries white people used. They could not drink from the same water fountains. They could not sit next to white people in movie the-

Jim Crow signs were everywhere.

aters. Usually they had to sit upstairs in the balcony. One law even said that blacks had to sit in the back of buses.

The laws kept blacks and whites apart. This was called "segregation."

M. L.'s mother told him not to think about the Jim Crow laws. They were bad.

They made life hard. But he should never think whites were better than blacks.

"You are just as good as anyone," she said.

M. L.'s father hated the laws. He tried very hard to fight segregation. He would not ride Atlanta buses. He kept away from segregated stores. But that was not always possible.

One time he took M. L. to buy some shoes. They walked into a store and sat down near the front. A white salesman came over and told them to go to the back. The seats in the front were for whites.

M. L.'s father got very angry. He turned to the white man. "We'll either buy shoes sitting here, or we won't buy shoes at all!" he said. Then he took M. L. by the hand and marched out of the store.

M. L. never forgot how much his father hated the Jim Crow laws.

4

School Days

M. L. was small. But he was so smart that his mother let him go to school a year early. There were no kindergartens in Atlanta public schools.

Rebecca Dickenson, the first-grade teacher, was a friend of M. L.'s mother. She agreed to let him try. He was a year younger than the rest of the children. But he became the best reader in the class.

He loved school and loved sports. It didn't matter that he was small. He played just as hard as the bigger boys.

When he got to high school, he played fullback on the football team. He was on the basketball team. He was good at wrestling as well as team sports.

*M. L. (front row, 4th from left) at a birthday party
with his friends.*

Most of his friends called him Mike or
Martin as he grew up. But he was still M. L.
at home.

Martin liked to dance. He also liked to

14

dress well. His high school friends called him "Tweed" because he had a tweed sport jacket. Tweed is a rough woolen material.

And he still loved words. Reading was easy for him. He wrote excellent reports and funny stories. He got very far ahead of his class. He skipped both the ninth and the twelfth grades.

Martin used words in many ways. At a young age he decided to win fights by talking instead of hitting.

And he could speak well in front of many people. He practiced giving speeches in front of a mirror. When he was 15, he won an important speaking contest in Atlanta.

One time Martin and some other students went to a speaking contest out of town. It was a long trip.

Martin's voice had changed. It had become rich and deep. He had practiced reading a speech he had written. The speech was called "The Negro and the Constitu-tion." It sounded good to M. L. But how would it sound to the judges?

The judges gave him a prize. Martin and his friends were excited. Mrs. Bradley, their teacher, was very happy. On the way back the bus was filled with people. But the boys found seats at last.

Then some white people got on. The bus driver turned around. He told Martin and the other black students to stand up and give their seats to the white people. That was the law.

Martin and his friends knew this was unfair. Why should they give their seats to someone else? They had paid just as much for the ride. They did not move. This made the bus driver very angry. He yelled at them. He called them awful names.

Martin's teacher told the boys to obey the law. So they stood up and let white people take their seats. Martin was furious. They had to stand for about two hours. He had never been so angry in his life. It was hard not to hate all white people.

Now Martin hated the Jim Crow laws as much as his father did. But what could he do to fight them?

5

Gandhi's Way

Martin started at Morehouse College, in Atlanta, when he was just 15. Both his father and grandfather had gone there. Many famous black men were Morehouse graduates.

Martin never missed a class. He read, listened, and discussed new ideas.

Martin was not quite sure what he wanted to be. He did know that he wanted to serve black Americans. But how? He thought about becoming a lawyer. Or perhaps a doctor. His mother thought that was a good choice. During high school he was sure of one thing. He did not want to be a minister like his father. But at Morehouse he changed his mind about it.

He studied the life and writings of Henry David Thoreau. Thoreau had been an American thinker with different ideas. He believed that people should not follow unjust laws. Thoreau felt slavery was unjust. He refused to pay taxes and went to jail to show he was against slavery. Martin thought more black people should know about Thoreau's ideas.

People listened when a minister spoke. Maybe as a minister he could do more to help black people.

Martin's father was pleased. But he didn't tell Martin. He asked his son to speak in church, to see how well he could do. It was Martin's first sermon. He was only 17.

Martin began to speak in the small room of the church. More and more people crowded in to hear him. Soon everyone had to move to the big hall.

Martin gave a very good sermon. His par-

Martin preaching at his father's church.

ents were very proud. A church member said, "We felt the Lord had laid his hands upon him."

In the summer Martin worked. But he did not get jobs that paid well. And he soon learned an important lesson. Blacks were paid less than whites for equal work. He loaded trains and trucks. He did hard work in factories. These were the jobs most black men did. Martin wanted to live the hard life of black working men. Maybe he could see a way to make life better for them.

After Morehouse, Martin went to a special college for ministers. It was Crozer College in Pennsylvania.

There were no Jim Crow laws in Pennsylvania. At Crozer, Martin went to school with white people for the first time. He liked some of them very much. He saw that there were different kinds of white people. There were only half a dozen black students at Crozer. But Martin was elected president of the student body.

At Crozer Martin learned about Mohandas Gandhi. He had led India to independence from British rule. Gandhi had also studied Thoreau. Like Martin, Gandhi had

Gandhi led his country to freedom by peaceful means.

lived under cruel and unfair laws. But he and his people found a way to fight these laws. They simply broke them. When the police threw them in jail, they didn't fight back.

This way of fighting was called "passive resistance."

Soon the jails of India were filled. There was no one left to do the work. At last the leaders had to change the laws to get the country going again. Gandhi was patient. He used passive resistance. He went on long fasts, when he did not eat for months. His fame spread throughout the world. At last he won independence for India. And he had won it without hurting or killing people.

Martin read more and more about Gandhi. Could Gandhi's way work against the Jim Crow laws?

6

Three Choices

Martin was the best student in his class at Crozer. When he graduated, he won an award of $1200 to go to another college.

He chose Boston University, in Massachusetts. He wanted to study the ideas of more great thinkers. What had they said about how people should live?

Martin and his friends liked to discuss these ideas. They met for coffee in the apartment Martin shared with a friend from Morehouse. At first they formed a club for black men. But soon both white students and women joined them. They talked of ways to make life better for all people.

Martin had many friends, black and

white, in Boston. But he had no favorite girl-friend. Then a friend told him of a lovely young woman from Alabama. Her name was Coretta Scott. She was studying to be a singer.

They made a date to have lunch between her classes at music school. The day they met, Martin could not stop looking at Coretta. She was very beautiful and she was very smart. He could share his ideas with her. They talked and talked.

"You're everything I'm looking for in a wife," he told Coretta. They began to spend every spare moment together. They went to concerts and took long walks. Coretta cared about the rights of black people as much as Martin did. Soon he asked her to marry him.

It was hard for Coretta to decide. She was a very good singer. She had planned to sing in concert halls all over the country. If she married, she might have to give up her singing. She wondered if she loved Martin enough to do it. At last she decided that she did.

On June 18, 1953, Martin and Coretta were married in Alabama. Martin's father performed the ceremony. His brother, A. D., was the best man.

Martin and Coretta finished their studies in Boston. It was time to decide what to do. They had many friends in Boston. They had black friends and white friends. And Boston was in the North, where there were no Jim Crow laws. Life might be better for them there.

Several colleges offered Martin teaching jobs. Some churches in the North asked Martin to be their minister. It would be easier to live in the North. But Martin said no. He wanted to help black people. The place to start was in the South, where life was hardest for them.

Martin took a job as the pastor of the Dexter Avenue Church. It was a small church in Montgomery, Alabama. But many of the black doctors, lawyers, and business people belonged to it. In May, the Kings settled in a

Martin became the pastor at Dexter Avenue Church.

big white house near the Dexter Avenue Church.

On Sundays, Martin preached at the church and Coretta sang in the choir. Martin visited the sick. He helped the poor. He spoke up about unjust laws. Soon he was an important leader in Montgomery.

Montgomery was a segregated city, like Atlanta. There were lots of Jim Crow laws. Whites and blacks went to different schools. They rode in different taxis. They went to different churches. Martin met with blacks who wanted to fight against segregation. They talked about taxis and about schools.

But most of all they talked about the city buses.

All bus riders, black and white, paid at the front door. They paid the same amount. But often only the whites got to sit down.

All the drivers were white. They made the black riders climb off the bus after they paid.

Montgomery, Alabama, was a Jim Crow city.

Then they had to walk to the rear door and climb back on. Only then could they sit down. That is, if the driver did not pull away with the rider's money before he or she could get on again. And if white people wanted the seats in the back, the blacks could not sit down at all.

Some drivers were rude to black people. They called them "niggers" and other terrible names.

Blacks hated to ride the city buses. Each time they paid their fares, they were reminded that they were second-class citizens. But they had to get to work. What else could they do?

7

Rosa Parks

On December 1, 1955, a black woman named Rosa Parks did something about the Jim Crow buses.

Mrs. Parks worked in a department store. That evening she climbed on a bus and sat down.

Each time the bus stopped, more people got on. Soon no seats were left in the white part of the bus.

At the next stop some white people got on. The driver got up and walked over to Rosa Parks. He told her to give her seat to a white person.

But Rosa Parks was tired. Her feet hurt. She did something she had never done before. She just stayed in her seat.

Again the driver told Rosa Parks to get up. But she would not move.

The driver was furious. He called a policeman. He told him that a black woman would not give up her seat.

Rosa Parks decided not to give up her seat.

The police fingerprint Rosa Parks.

The policeman pulled Mrs. Parks off the bus. He took her to the police station. The police took her fingerprints and threw her in jail. All because she was tired and didn't want to get up!

Black people all over the city heard about

Rosa Parks. They were very angry. They were mad at the Jim Crow laws. They were mad at the police. They were mad at the bus company. But what could they do?

Then one man said, "Why don't we boycott the buses?" This meant that all the black people would stop riding the buses. Soon the bus company would lose money. Maybe then the owners would be fair to blacks.

Boycott! The word spread like wildfire. Someone called Martin Luther King. He liked the idea right away.

But a boycott would work only if *all* the blacks stayed off the buses. How could the leaders get word to every black person in Montgomery in time?

Martin and the others worked fast. They wrote a flier about the boycott. They gave copies away in every part of the city where black people lived. But they could not reach everybody.

Could they reach enough to make the boycott work?

Then they had some good luck. A black maid got a copy of the flier. She could not read well. So she showed it to the white woman she worked for. The woman read the note. It made her very angry. How dare those blacks boycott the buses! She called the Montgomery newspaper and told the editor about the boycott plan.

The editor of the paper got angry too. He wrote a story about the boycott. The story was printed on the first page of the newspaper. And the flier was printed word for word!

Many blacks saw the story in the paper. The paper was against the boycott. But it helped to make the boycott a success.

The night before the boycott, the Kings were up late. Their new baby, Yolanda, was crying. At last she was quiet. But her parents stayed awake worrying about tomorrow.

Would the boycott work?

Morning came. Coretta looked out the window at the bus stop. Soon the first bus of the day rolled up. On most days it was filled with black people.

"Martin! Martin! Come quickly!" Coretta cried.

Martin ran to the window. The bus was empty! He wanted to shout with joy.

Another empty bus drove by. And then another. The boycott was working!

8

The Boycott Gets
a Leader

All day long empty buses rolled through the streets of Montgomery. Black people all over the city joined the boycott. Some walked to work. Some rode on mules or in wagons. Some rode bicycles. Each fought the Jim Crow laws in his or her own way.

The people who had planned the boycott held a meeting in the afternoon. Martin Luther King was elected president of the group. The group would be called the Montgomery Improvement Association, or MIA.

That night there was an open meeting in the Holt Street Baptist Church. The MIA had expected a few hundred people to attend.

But the church was packed. Four thousand more crowded around outside the church. They wanted to know what would happen. Loudspeakers were set up so they could hear.

Should the boycott go on? The day had been a great success. The black citizens of Montgomery had shown they could unite for a just cause. It was hard to walk to work. It was hard to ride a mule to a store. But it was the only way to fight the Jim Crow laws.

The people voted. Those who wanted to keep the boycott going were asked to stand.

All through the crowded church people rose to their feet. They looked around. Everyone there was standing! All the blacks were willing to stay off the buses. A cheer went up. The boycott would continue!

Martin Luther King stood up to speak. He knew he must speak well. Black people in Montgomery were doing a brave and dangerous thing. And they trusted him to lead them.

"There comes a time when people get tired," he said. "We are here this evening to say we are tired of being kicked about."

Everyone cheered wildly. The bus boycott would continue. And the black citizens of Montgomery had a leader!

People got places however they could.

9

The Whites
Get Tough

The boycott went straight through into January. Black people still walked. They still rode mules and shared cars.

People all over the country—both black and white—sent money to help the boycott in Montgomery. Martin and the MIA began to round up hundreds of cars. Black people began to drive each other to work in car pools. White and black airmen from a near-by airbase helped too.

Now white people in Montgomery were angry. The men who ran the bus company were furious. They were losing money. They wanted the boycott stopped. The mayor hated it. He told the police to get tough with the boycott leaders.

The police did get tough. And the first person they got tough with was Martin Luther King, Jr.

One day Martin was driving his car down the street. All at once two white policemen stopped him.

"Get out, King," they said. "You're under arrest for driving 30 miles an hour in a 25-mile zone."

Martin knew they were wrong. But he had to obey. They pushed him into their car and drove him to jail.

The news spread fast. Soon a large crowd of angry blacks had gathered outside the jail. The jailer was afraid they might break in. He set King free. But King did not stay out of jail long. The police arrested him again and again.

The police were not the only ones who

tried to stop King. One night Martin spoke at a meeting. Coretta stayed home, talking to a friend.

A car roared past the house. A man in the car threw something out. Coretta heard a loud thump on the porch. She thought some-

The police arrest King.

one must have thrown a brick. But she was worried. She grabbed the baby and led her friend to the back of the house.

Just then there was an explosion! It was a bomb! The bomb blew a big hole in the porch. Most of the front windows were broken. But no one was hurt.

Someone rushed to tell Martin.

The explosion was so loud that it was heard from blocks away. Soon a crowd of angry black people stood in front of the house. White policemen drove up and told them to go home. But they would not move. When the mayor came, the crowd muttered in anger.

King arrived and spoke to the crowd.

"Don't get panicky," he said. "If you have weapons, take them home. We must meet our white brothers' hate with love."

He told them others would try to stop him. But still black people must use peaceful ways to fight for freedom. "If I am stopped, our work will not stop. For what we are doing is right!"

"God bless you, son!" someone cried. Slowly the crowd broke up.

Someone had tried to kill Martin Luther King, but he had talked of love! The police were amazed. "I owe my life to that nigger preacher," said one of them.

10
Victory

It was March. The battle of the buses dragged on.

The white leaders of Mongomery decided to try something new. They arrested the boycott leaders for stopping the bus company's business.

Martin Luther King went to court. He was found guilty and fined $500. But he didn't mind. Money would come from somewhere. He knew his fight for justice could not be stopped.

And so did his people. A big crowd cheered him as he left the court. "Long live the King!" they cried.

Eight months later, Martin Luther King

sat in court again. It was November 13, 1956. White leaders had a new plan. They said the MIA car pools took business from the bus company. They asked the judge to say that the car pools were against the law.

King was worried. It looked as if the judge would make the MIA give up the car pools. Then the boycott would have to end. Black people would have to ride Jim Crow buses again. The fight would be lost!

Martin felt sad as he sat in court. Suddenly a reporter handed him a note. It was exciting news from the United States Supreme Court. The Supreme Court is the most important court in America. What it says is more important than what any state courts say. And now the Supreme Court had said segregation in city buses was against the law!

King could hardly believe it. The black people had won! Jim Crow buses would be

King's supporters cheered as he left the courthouse.

gone forever from Montgomery. And they would be gone from every other city in the United States.

On December 21, 1956, King stood at a bus stop with other boycott leaders. Soon a bus pulled up.

As Martin Luther King climbed on, the driver said, "We're glad to have you this morning."

King smiled and walked to a seat near the front.

11

SCLC

Black Americans had beaten the Jim Crow bus laws. Why not fight the other segregation laws?

Martin Luther King, Jr., and other black ministers of the South met in Atlanta. They formed a new group to fight segregation. It was called the Southern Christian Leadership Conference, or SCLC. And Martin Luther King was elected president.

In speech after speech, King told black people how to fight. He urged them to act with "calm and loving dignity." He told them not to obey unfair laws. He said to go to places Jim Crow laws said they could not go. And to do things unfair laws said not to do. If police came to take them to jail, they should go quietly. Even if people hurt them, they must hurt no one.

"We must have the courage to refuse to fight back," he said. "We must use the weapon of love."

He believed white leaders would get tired of all the trouble and change the laws. This was the way Gandhi had won.

SCLC had other work, too. All over the South, whites kept black citizens from voting. Black people couldn't elect local leaders or even vote for president. This was unjust. Every American was supposed to have the right to vote. Now SCLC would fight to bring that basic right to the five million black Americans who lived in the South.

SCLC had sounded its battle cry. A peaceful war against segregation had begun.

For two years King led the voting drive. He ran meetings and gave speeches. He wrote a book about the boycott. And he kept working at the Dexter Avenue Church.

Martin Luther King, Jr., loved all of the members of his church. He had shared a great struggle with the black people of Montgomery. But he knew it was time to move on.

One Sunday King asked everyone to stay after church services. He told them he must leave. He needed more time to work for SCLC. Black people all over America needed his help. He had become the leader of their fight for freedom. He would go to Atlanta and work in his father's church.

The people were very sad. They hated to let their great minister go. But they knew it was right.

At the end he asked them to join hands and sing a hymn with him. And as the music filled the church he loved, Martin Luther King broke down and cried.

12

The Sit-ins

From Ebenezer Baptist Church in Atlanta, King spoke out to black people everywhere. He called upon them to fight for their freedom. He gave them hope and courage. More and more blacks took up the fight against segregation in America. And more and more whites joined them.

One afternoon in February 1960, four black students marched into a Woolworth's store in Greensboro, North Carolina. They were neatly dressed and polite. They sat down at the Jim Crow lunch counter. They asked to buy food.

Many white people in the store were shocked and angry. The waitress would not

The sit-ins were a test of passive resistance.

serve them. Other whites shouted bad names at them.

But the young blacks pretended not to hear. They just sat quietly.

The next day they came back again. Still they were not served. So they came back another day. They said they would keep coming back until they were served.

There had been some "sit-ins" before in Baltimore and other Southern cities. But now they began in the Deep South.

Soon blacks started sit-ins in 14 other Southern cities. White students joined them. But many Southerners hated the sit-ins. They

Once again Martin is in jail.

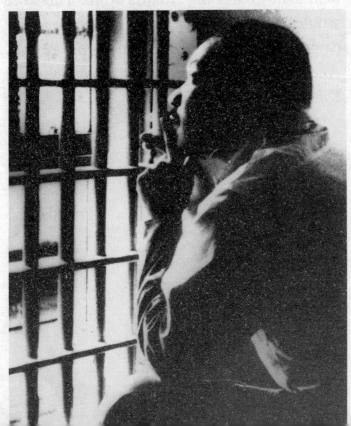

tried to stop them. They beat the students. They burned them with cigarettes.

But day after day the young people came back. And at last some of the Jim Crow stores gave up. They agreed to let black people eat at their lunch counters.

Black Americans had won another great battle against Jim Crow.

In October 1960 King and a large group held a sit-in at a big Atlanta store. The store would not serve them food. Soon the police came. They arrested more than 50 people. And that night, once again, Martin Luther King slept behind bars.

13

Freedom Rides

After the sit-ins came "freedom rides." In the South some of the big buses traveling from state to state were still segregated. Freedom rides were sit-ins on these buses.

On May 4, 1961, two Greyhound buses left Washington, D.C. They headed south. Thirteen freedom riders were on board. At every stop they sat at lunch counters marked "whites only." They used "white" waiting rooms. And on the buses they always sat near the front.

What would happen? All over the country people waited for the news. They were glued to their TV sets.

The trip began quietly. Then, in Alabama,

The freedom riders' burning bus.

some white people cut the tires of the first bus. They followed the bus out of town.

Soon the tires went flat. When the bus stopped, the white people set it on fire. As the frightened riders ran out, the whites attacked them. The group had to give up the trip. But another group took over. Soon, however, they too were attacked.

The next night the freedom riders held a huge meeting in a church in Montgomery. Martin Luther King rushed to Montgomery to speak.

While he spoke, a crowd of angry white people tried to break into the church. King asked his people to sing the black freedom song "We Shall Overcome." As stones and bottles hit the church, the blacks inside sang, "We are not afraid." At last soldiers sent the crowd home.

In the next days a new group began to plan more freedom rides. King was one of the leaders.

For months the rides went on. TV crews followed them. The whole world watched. Support for the freedom riders grew stronger and stronger. At last the U.S. government sent out an order. It said segregation in all buses, trains, and waiting rooms was against the law. The freedom riders had won!

Some whites hated the idea of integration.

King had a new plan. Sit-ins at lunch counters and on buses had worked. Why not a sit-in for a whole city?

In December of 1961 freedom riders were arrested in Albany, Georgia. King began a great sit-in to end *all* the segregation laws in Albany. For months he led marches. He led sit-ins all over the city. But somehow nothing happened. White leaders didn't change the laws. The black people gave up. It was the first time Martin Luther King had lost a fight.

14

Birmingham

Martin Luther King did not win in Albany. But he learned something there. He learned he could not fight a whole city with only a few hundred people. He needed an army.

He needed thousands of Americans to march against Jim Crow. He needed thousands who were not afraid to go to jail. And still more thousands to keep marching. He would show the whole country how much black people hated segregation. He would make white leaders see that they had to end the Jim Crow laws.

Where would he find such an army? Where would he fight his next battle? He picked Birmingham, Alabama. Birmingham

Police dogs attack a marcher.

was known as the worst Jim Crow city in America.

In April 1963 King led a group of 40 marchers toward city hall. They would demand to talk to white leaders.

On they came. A thousand blacks lined the street, shouting "Freedom has come to Birmingham!"

The police were waiting. Their chief was a tough white man named Bull Connor. He made life hard for the black people of Birmingham.

Bull Connor watched the marchers coming. "Stop 'em!" he shouted. The police moved in. They rounded the marchers up and threw them in jail.

Whenever King was put in jail, he called Coretta right away. But this time he did not call. Two days passed. Coretta was very worried.

Then, at last, a call came. But it wasn't

from Martin. It was from John F. Kennedy, the president of the United States.

"I wanted you to know," he said, "that I have talked with Birmingham. I have arranged for your husband to call you." He told her that Martin was all right. It was wonderful news for Coretta.

Soon King was out of jail and marching again. Each day more people marched with him. And each day the police got tougher. They beat the blacks with clubs. They used fierce police dogs to attack the marchers. They turned fire hoses on them. The water hit like a hammer. It was so strong, that it smashed the marchers to the ground.

The marchers kept on using passive resistance. The world watched. More and more people supported the cause of freedom.

Then King decided on a dangerous plan. There would be a children's march. He didn't

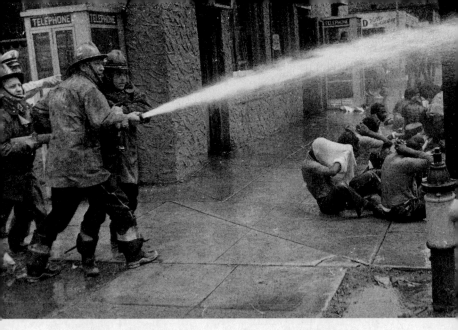

The police turned strong fire hoses on the marchers.

think police could be cruel enough to attack young children.

The black children of Birmingham gathered one morning in May. They began to march. And as they marched, they sang, "Deep in my heart, I do believe, we shall overcome someday."

Bull Connor's police blocked off the street. They waited. The singing children marched toward them. Then the police hit them with everything they had—hoses, dogs, clubs. They packed a thousand children off to jail. Some were only six years old.

The blacks of Birmingham could hardly believe it. The rest of the country could not believe it either. What kind of men could put a six-year-old in jail? They rose in fury. Now thousands upon thousands marched against segregation in Birmingham.

The men who ran the city could take it no longer. On Friday, May 10, they met with black leaders. They promised to end the Jim Crow laws. Freedom had come to Birmingham!

15

"I Have a Dream"

All over America black people watched the news from Birmingham. They said, "If blacks are brave enough to march in Birmingham, we can march too."

Now blacks marched everywhere. More whites joined them. During the long, hot summer of 1963, the crowds grew bigger. Where once there were just hundreds of marchers, now there were thousands. Where once there were thousands, now there were hundreds of thousands.

They marched and sang in more than 800 cities. They marched for the end of unfair laws. They shouted for the end of segregation. They cried out for freedom.

The March on Washington, August 28, 1963.

And then on August 28, 1963, Martin Luther King and other black leaders marched right into Washington, D.C. Over 250,000 people marched with them. They came from all over the country. They came by train and plane. They came by bus, by car, and on foot.

Most of the crowd was black. But there were thousands of whites. They wanted to show that they hated segregation too. They wanted to join the fight for freedom.

A sea of peaceful protestors.

It was not an angry crowd. The people were proud and happy. They sang songs and listened to speeches.

Many black leaders gave fine speeches. But Martin Luther King gave a speech America will never forget.

"I have a dream today!" His voice shook with feeling. Someday, he said, "little black boys and little black girls will join hands with little white boys and white girls and walk together as sisters and brothers.

"I have a dream today!"

A cheer went up from the crowd. Someday, King went on, *all* God's children would join hands. Together they would sing the words of the old black song, "Free at last, free at last. Thank God Almighty, we are free at last!"

When he finished, many of the marchers were crying. They stood and cheered Martin Luther King. Then everyone joined hands, blacks and whites together, and sang "We Shall Overcome." It was a day that will never be forgotten by anyone who was there. It was a day of high hope.

But less than three weeks later a bomb was thrown into a Baptist church in Alabama. It killed four little girls. It hurt 21 other children. Black Americans were not even safe in church. The country was shocked.

The governor of Alabama was against integrating the schools. His speeches were full of hate. King blamed the governor for the violence. At the memorial service King tried to quiet the anger blacks felt with hope. "The children did not die in vain," he said. "God still has a way of wringing good from evil."

Then violence struck again. President John F. Kennedy was killed in Dallas, Texas. He had fought hard for a civil rights bill.

The vice-president, Lyndon Johnson,

became the president. In his first speech to Congress, he asked the lawmakers to honor the memory of President Kennedy. The best way they could do it was by passing the civil rights bill. He urged them to do it as soon as possible.

President Johnson signing the Civil Rights Act.

In 1964, President Johnson signed the Civil Rights Act. Martin Luther King, Jr., stood right behind him. It was a great victory. But it did not assure the voting rights of all Americans. Martin knew he would have to keep on marching.

16

The Nobel Prize

Martin Luther King was a famous man. He spoke and worked all around the country. But he tried to be with his family as much as he could.

Mrs. King worked for freedom too. Whenever she could, she marched at her husband's side.

The Kings had four children now. There were two boys, Martin and Dexter, and two girls, Yolanda and Bernice. They loved to play with their father. Somehow he found time to pitch a baseball, push a swing, and roughhouse with them.

Martin Luther King was often in jail. This was hard for the children to understand.

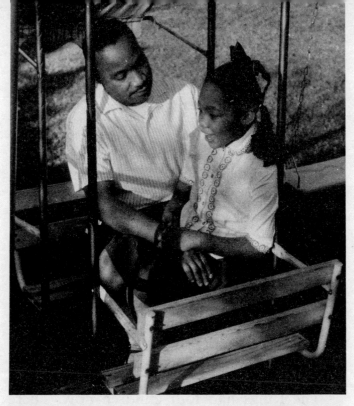

Martin with his daughter Yolanda.

"Your daddy went to jail to help people,"
Mrs. King once said. Soon after, Yolanda
heard on television that her father was in jail
again. She burst into tears. "Don't cry,
Yoki," said little Martin. "Daddy's gone to
help *more* people."

One of the most important prizes in the world is the Nobel Peace Prize. Every year the country of Norway gives it to the person who has done the most for peace.

Martin pitching a ball to his son Marty.

Martin receiving the Nobel Peace Prize.

In October of 1964 the Norwegian government sent out an exciting announcement. Martin Luther King, Jr., had won the Nobel Peace Prize! He was the youngest person ever to receive it.

King flew to Oslo, Norway, to accept the

prize. His whole family and many black leaders made the trip. The prize was a medal and $54,000. King gave the money to several civil rights groups. He said it belonged to all the men and women who had worked for freedom by using nonviolence.

He said the prize was not just for him. It was for "all men who love peace and brotherhood."

Then the Kings traveled around Europe. They met important leaders. Crowds cheered them. Governments honored them. But soon they left for home. They had work to do.

He spoke to a packed church when he came back. "I have been to the mountaintop," he said. "I really wish I could stay. But I must go back to the valley....There are people starving in the valley....There are those who need hope....And I *still* have a dream."

17

Selma and the North

Martin Luther King stopped to rest his feet. He was leading 650 people on a long, hard march from Selma, Alabama, to Montgomery, the state capital.

For weeks King had been working for fair voting laws in Selma. A young black working with him had been shot by a policeman. King had called on his people to march. They would show that blacks would risk their lives for the right to vote.

Many priests, rabbis, ministers, and other white people from the North had joined the march. King knew the march would be dangerous.

Priests, rabbis, and ministers marching with King.

"I can't promise that it won't get you beaten," he told his people. "I can't promise that it won't get your house bombed. But we must stand up for what is right."

It was a 50-mile march. Twice the marchers had tried to get through. Police met them on the road with whips. They knocked them down and trampled them with their horses.

Then President Johnson sent soldiers to protect the marchers. But two would never

Marchers on the way from Selma to Montgomery.

march again. A young minister was beaten to death by an Alabama mob. Later a white woman from the North was shot and killed.

But the others marched on, mile after mile. And at last, on March 25, 1965, they reached Montgomery. King spoke to his people. How long would they have to wait for freedom? "Not long," he said. "Because no lie can live forever." And segregation was a lie.

Soon after, the U.S. Congress passed a voting rights bill. President Johnson signed it. Millions of blacks could vote at last! Now King turned north. He began to work in the city of Chicago.

There were no Jim Crow laws in Northern cities. But black people still had problems. Many whites would not rent to blacks. And most blacks were poor. So they had to

Police blocking the marchers.

live in slums. In Chicago more than 800,000 blacks lived in row upon row of dirty buildings. There were rats and bugs. And often no heat.

King helped blacks in Chicago form groups. They tried to make owners clean up the buildings and give them heat.

He led many marches for "open housing." The marchers were pelted with stones and bricks. At last Chicago leaders signed an agreement. It said owners could not refuse to rent to blacks.

Now King carried the fight to other cities in the North.

18

Tired of Waiting

Martin Luther King had carried the fight around the country. And slowly life was getting better for some black people. The United States had passed civil rights laws. But states like Alabama and Mississippi did not obey them.

And now the civil rights movement faced a new problem. This time it did not come from whites. It came from other blacks.

In August of 1965, Watts, a neighborhood in Los Angeles, California, exploded. Rioting mobs of angry blacks broke into stores and stole things. They set fire to buildings, yelling, "Burn, baby, burn!"

When police couldn't stop them, soldiers

Watts, after the riots of 1965.

had to be called in. The rioting went on for six days. About 35 people were killed, and many more were hurt. A wave of fear swept over the country.

Blacks were sick and tired of waiting for a better life. They were tired of slums and Jim Crow, tired of bad jobs and poor pay. And they were tired of hearing Martin Luther King asking them to be patient.

Blacks had been stoned, bombed, and shot to death in the fight for freedom. Even their white supporters had been killed and beaten. Shouldn't they fight back?

Now many black people listened to new leaders, younger and louder than King. One of them, Stokely Carmichael, said the answer was "Black Power." He said, "We don't need...white phonies and liberals." Blacks should stick together to be strong, he argued. Some of these new leaders wanted to break away and start a new country. Others wanted to return violence with violence.

The National Association for the Advancement of Colored People (NAACP) was the oldest organization in the civil rights movement. It had many white members and supporters. The NAACP could not go along with the idea of black separation. For years the NAACP had worked for integration.

Other black organizations that had united

in the civil rights movement were divided on the idea of Black Power and the use of force. Martin Luther King, Jr., worked hard to keep the movement together. He would not give up his belief in "People Power" and nonviolence.

He understood that many of the young people calling for Black Power had lost hope. They had given up on nonviolence and passive resistance. The laws were better. But the will of those in power to enforce the laws was weak.

Stokely Carmichael calls for "Black Power."

President Johnson had denounced the Ku Klux Klan. That was the white group responsible for most of the killings, bombings, and beatings. But even when Klan members were arrested, they usually were let off.

The new bitterness of leaders like Stokely Carmichael upset King. If blacks followed them, there would be worse violence all over the country. He feared that riots might start in other cities. The conditions that had caused them had not changed.

King knew it was hard for his people to wait for freedom. He knew it took a long time to change bad habits. New laws were not enough. He agreed that America wasn't changing fast enough. But he asked his followers to use peaceful means to get what they wanted.

"Let us not despair," said King. "Let us not lose faith in man and certainly not in God. We must believe...that man...can be lifted from the valley of hate to the high mountain of love."

Fight harder, he said—but in a new way. Money is green. "Green Power—that's the kind of power we need," he said. "What good does it do to be able to eat at a lunch counter if you can't buy a hamburger?"

With more money, black people could have better houses and clothes and food. They could live better lives.

King began to plan a new march on Washington, a Poor People's March. The poor would demand better jobs and more pay. And the march would not just be for black people. It would be for *all* poor people, white and black.

King was busy planning the Poor People's March. On January 31, it was a rainy day in Memphis, Tennessee. When the garbage collectors came to work, they were sent home. White workers were paid for a full day's work. Black workers were paid for only two hours' work. The black union sent a list of their problems to the mayor of Memphis. He paid no attention to them. The union went on strike.

One of the Memphis leaders was the Reverend James Lawson. He was an old friend. The strike leaders wanted to have a march. Lawson asked King for help. He went to Memphis to help garbage collectors fight for equal treatment. He agreed to lead a march.

19

"I've Been to the Mountaintop"

A month before he went to Memphis, Martin Luther King spoke at Ebenezer Baptist Church.

People had tried to kill him. He knew he might die any day. So today he talked of his own death. If he were to die, what should be said at his funeral? He told his people that his prizes were not important. His schools were not important. What mattered was how he had lived his life.

Now, in Memphis, 6,000 people marched behind Martin Luther King. They would show the whole country that the peaceful way still worked.

King never lost his faith in nonviolence.

The march in Memphis.

King did not realize that many angry young people in Memphis believed Black Power was better than nonviolence. They called themselves the Invaders. Suddenly the Invaders began to smash windows. King demanded that the march be stopped. His followers listened and went home. The Invaders continued to break windows and loot stores. Soon a terrible riot began.

King's men rushed him to safety. The next day he left Memphis.

He was sad and upset. King had not planned the march. Yet he felt he had failed. Had the riot been his fault? He asked, "Am I doing any good?" He was afraid that there might be more riots. How could he stop them? He might go on a fast. He would stop eating to show black people how he felt about riots and talk of hate. Then perhaps they would listen to his call for peace. Gandhi had fasted in India. It had worked there.

Then King and his men knew what to do. On the way to the Poor People's March, they would go back to Memphis. A new march was set for April 8. Two of King's closest helpers were Jesse Jackson and Hosea Williams. They would give workshops in nonviolence to the people of Memphis. They would show they could win the fight *their* way.

Suddenly King wasn't worried anymore. He knew black people would be free one day. Hating and killing would stop, and peace would come.

On April 3, 1968, he returned to Memphis. That night there was a heavy rainstorm. There were tornado warnings. King went out into the storm to speak at a rally.

Memphis whites talked of killing him. But Martin Luther King wasn't afraid. He called them "our sick white brothers."

"Like anybody, I'd like to live a long life," he said. But living a long life didn't matter to him now. "I just want to do God's will." Ahead he saw a time of peace, the "Promised Land" of the Bible.

"I've been to the mountaintop," he said. "And I've seen the Promised Land. I may not

Martin outside his motel room with SCLC workers.

get there with you. But...we as a people will get to the Promised Land. So I'm happy tonight. I'm not worried about anything. I'm not fearing any man. Mine eyes have seen the glory of the coming of the Lord."

King spent most of the next day with his SCLC workers. He spoke about Gandhi and Jesus. He said nonviolence was the only hope for this country. He spoke to his closest aide, Ralph Abernathy. He told him never to let anyone who believed in violence join the SCLC staff.

That evening King stood on his motel porch. He was chatting with several friends who were in the parking lot below. At a window across the way a shadow moved. Suddenly a single shot rang out! King fell.

Within an hour he was dead.

20

"Drum Major for Justice"

President Johnson declared April 7 a day of national mourning. American flags were at half-mast.

All over the world people wept. More than 50,000 people came to the funeral in Atlanta. There were governors, senators, mayors, and justices of the Supreme Court. Black and white, rich and poor, young and old came to say good-bye to a great man.

In some way Martin Luther King, Jr., had helped them all. He had helped the poor and the sick. He had made black people really believe they were "as good as anyone." And he had helped to wake up white Americans.

He had shown them that people all over their country were still not free. He had shown that they, too, must work for fair laws and for peace.

He didn't care about money or fame. He didn't even think his Nobel Prize was important. To him, *justice* was important. He called himself a "drum major for justice."

It was important to obey laws. But only if they were fair laws. He went to jail 30 times fighting unjust laws.

Mules pulled the simple wagon that held his casket.

Coretta at the memorial services.

Martin Luther King dreamed that one day black and white children would join hands as sisters and brothers. He did not live to see his dream come true. But he had looked down from the mountaintop and seen the Promised Land. And he had shown Americans a way to get there.

21

Did the Dream Come True?

It has been 25 years since Martin Luther King, Jr., was killed.

On the surface it might seem that he died in vain. There are still many black Americans who do not have jobs. Drugs, which were a much smaller problem in King's time, have become a very serious problem. Drugs have hurt all Americans. But they have harmed young, poor people who live in cities more than any other group.

There seems to be less understanding and more fear between the races. Peace and the nonviolent ways that Martin Luther King, Jr., was willing to die for seem further away than ever.

But the news turns the spotlight on trouble rather than on quieter changes. It does not show us black and white families, who now live in integrated neighborhoods and apartment buildings. It does not show us black and white workers doing equal jobs and getting equal pay.

Let's look at some of the changes that would have made Martin smile.

Martin Luther King, Jr., watched President Johnson sign the Civil Rights Act in 1964. At that time there were about 300 black Americans who had been elected to public office in the *whole country*. By November 1968, the total rose to over 1,000. By 1993, the total was close to 8,000. Most of the growth is in the South. The first black governor was elected in Virginia in 1989. The Reverend Jesse Jackson ran for president in 1984 and again in 1988. Black and white Americans from all over the country voted for him.

And Martin Luther King, Jr., would certainly be pleased that many of those elected are women. In 1992, a black woman, Carol Moseley-Braun, was elected to the United States Senate.

There are black Americans in every branch of the federal government from the Congress to the Supreme Court. Black men and women report the news on television. Television shows the whole country that there are many outstanding black Americans. They can be seen in the military, business, and the sciences from medicine to the space program.

January 15, Martin Luther King's birthday, is now a national holiday. He is the only American who was not a president to be given this honor. It is a chance for all of us to remember his message of peace and freedom. It is a time for all people to think about bringing his dream closer.

Landmark Books® Grades 2 and Up

Landmark Books® Grades 4 and Up

Landmark Books® Grades 6 and Up